Rainbow Kids

Hawaii's Gift to America

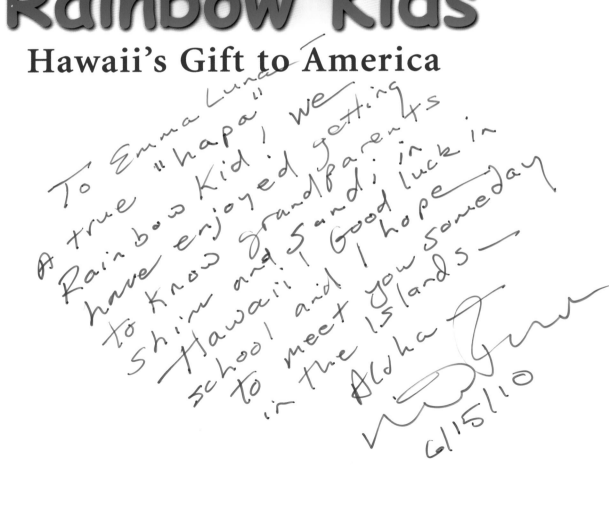

To Emma Luna —
A true "hapa"
Rainbow Kid! we
have enjoyed getting
to know grandparents
Shin and Sandi in
Hawaii! Good luck in
school and I hope someday
to meet you someday
in the Islands —
Aloha
6/15/10

Rainbow Kids

Hawaii's Gift to America

C. Richard Fassler

White Tiger Press

To my mother, Genevieve, and my sister, Judy, for their love and inspiration.

Acknowledgments

I would like to thank the following people who, in some important way, assisted *Rainbow Kids*: my parents, Carl and Genevieve Fassler of Sun City, Arizona, for their enthusiasm for their son's inter-racial marriage; my sister, Judy Arkebauer, of Sylvania, Ohio, who, like many Mainlanders, fell in love with Hawaii's kids and urged me to publish my photos; Jack Yuen, for gifts of cameras and sound advice on photography; Frank DeLima, Hawaii's favorite humorist, for providing the Foreword; Brook Lee, for permission to use her quote; Mrs. Andrew W. Lind, for permission to use her husband's introduction; Patrick Downes, for his help and encouragement; Pat Tomita, Maitland Rosa and Gary Lin of Photofinish Hawaii, for preparing my photos for publication; Warren Iwasa and Michael Walther, for guiding me through the publication process; Dick Lyday, for arranging the printing; Joan Clarke, author of *Family Traditions in Hawai'i*, for her many sound suggestions; my colleagues at the Aquaculture Development Program; and to all the Rainbow Kids and their families for allowing me to take their pictures.

Library of Congress Catalog Card Number: 98-090716

First Printing: December, 1998

ISBN: 0-9667064-0-4

Printed in Hong Kong

White Tiger Press
2112 Haena Drive
Honolulu, Hawaii 96822
Telephone: 808-946-7305
Email: kimber@hgea.org

Contents

Foreword   6

Introduction   9

Kimo Dan Francisco Chan, a poem   13

Introduction to *Hawaiian Types*   91

Kids' Quiz   93

Kids' Quiz Answers   94

About the poet/photographer   96

Cover: Haley
Title page: Denise with flowers. Introduction: Leslie
Above, left to right: Denise, Jaime, Kimi; Amy; Kory, Andrew, Alvaro and Ryan M.;
Emma; Jaime and Kimi; Kristoria

Foreword

by Frank DeLima

As an entertainer in Hawaii who draws on the rich ethnic heritage of our Islands as a source of material both comic and musical, I am especially pleased to introduce this book to you.

Rainbow Kids, with Richard Fassler's wonderful photos, proves once again that the phrase "there is no place like Hawaii" is not just some advertising slogan or song lyric cliché--it's the God's truth. Because, while the Islands have an abundance of natural beauty, its people are like no other people on earth. For here, different races and different peoples have melded into a new race and a new people, one which bears the future face of humanity.

You will see this face again and again in the pages of this book. It is the product of inter-racial harmony, respect and love. It is the face of Hawaii's children.

You really don't need a book to demonstrate that the multi-ethnic child is Hawaii's gift to America, and the rest of the world. A walk along the beach, down an Island street, or through a neighborhood playground, will verify it for you. And if you don't believe your eyes, check the statistics: they show that the majority of people born in Hawaii today are of mixed ethnic heritage. No other place can make that claim.

I used to joke that, here in Hawaii, no matter how "ugly" the parents are, if they are of different races, the kids will turn out cute. There is actually enough truth to that statement that people will laugh when I say it! They've seen it. They can relate. I personally think that cute children is God's wondrous way of rewarding us for loving each other and getting along.

In Hawaii, we use the word *hapa* or "half" to describe those of mixed ancestry. The word is generally paired with the word *haole*, or Caucasian, as in *hapa-haole*, or half-white. But in reality, "half" is only the smallest division one needs to qualify as *hapa*.

I believe that if there is a racial recipe for beauty, the more ingredients the better. Take the classic ethnic features--the chiseled angularity of the Caucasian, the soft roundness of the Asian, the smooth symmetry of the Polynesian, the full expressiveness of the African--what could be more interesting than to mix them up? Blend the colors of skin, eyes and hair, and the result is golden.

Look closely at the faces in this book. They are interesting, fascinating, full of mystery and charm, each hinting at exotic stories of far-off lands, foreign languages, and distant shores, of journeying ancestors, and adventurous romances. Look! A green-eyed Hawaiian! A red-haired Japanese! A freckled Chinese! Over there--she's Filipino, English, Chinese, Irish, Spanish! Over here–he's Hawaiian, Portuguese, Japanese, German!

As an Island comedian, much of my humor is derived from our ethnic identities. So, in the context of our calabash culture, I will poke fun at the idiosyncrasies of the Chinese, the Hawaiians, the Filipinos, the Japanese, the Portuguese, the haoles,

Frank (8th Grade)

• Portuguese • Scottish • English
• Hawaiian • Irish • Chinese

the Samoans, the Blacks and so on. One of the reasons I can get away with this (only in Hawaii) without being labeled horribly politically incorrect is that the person to whom I might direct my humor is very likely to be Japanese-Korean-Irish, married to a German-Hawaiian-Samoan, whose godmother is Filipino-Spanish, and whose brother-in-law is Portuguese-Scottish-English-Hawaiian-Irish-Chinese (my background, by the way).

In other words, we are literally laughing at ourselves--not at other groups. Our ethnic humor differs radically from that of other places because it aims to unite rather than divide, to be familiar rather than hostile, to tickle rather than punch.

Which brings me back to the Rainbow Kids. We are blessed with them because the people who are native to these Islands and those who came here from cultures and lands far away did more than respect each other, or appreciate and admire each other. They fell in love.

And as a result, they made a beautiful place more beautiful still.

Introduction

"This island (state) represents all that we are and all that we hope to become."

John F. Kennedy, Honolulu, Hawaii, June, 1963

◆ ◆ ◆ ◆

(Being Miss Universe) "is about being open to a lot of different cultures. I've been to thirteen different countries in a year, and wherever I go, they think I'm that ethnicity. So it's about being able to accept people for whatever they are. In Hawaii, we're like that by nature. I'm Hawaiian, Korean, Chinese, Dutch, English, French, Portuguese. So they all had to get along for me to be born!"

Brook Mahealani Lee, Miss Universe, on The Oprah Winfrey Show, May 7, 1998

"What are you?"

The answer to that question is likely to confound someone from the Mainland United States. Hawaii residents, however, like Brook Lee, will quickly reply with a list of nationalities from the four corners of the world.

This state, you see, is highly unique. Nowhere in the U.S., and possibly nowhere among the major population centers of the world, is there a higher percentage of persons of mixed European, African, Asian and Polynesian ancestry than in Hawaii. And, perhaps nowhere on the face of this earth have so many different people lived together so peacefully for so long.

Persons from many nations and Hawaiians have met and married in the Islands for the past century-and-a-half, and the state continues to extend a warm *aloha* for all who wish to reside here.

Stigmas against interracial marriage are practically non-existent.

Fifty years ago, nearly 1/4 of the children born in Hawaii were of mixed racial ancestry. The 1990 census revealed that the number of persons in the state considered "mixed" was 421,461--more than 1/3 of the total population. It appears likely that the majority of Island residents born in the early part of the next century will fall into that category.

On a stopover to the Islands in June, 1963, a lei-bedecked President John Kennedy told his welcomers that Hawaii "represents all that we are and all that we hope to become." The nation had passed through a period of severe racial strife and more was to come. He sensed that this state provided an example of a multiracial population living in harmony that the rest of the country would do well to imitate.

The president's wish is coming true. Over the past two decades, the Mainland United States has become much more cosmopolitan. Today, Asian-born Americans outnumber those born in Europe. Indeed, they are the fastest growing ethnic group in the U.S. and their population is expected to double to 20 million in the next century. In Los Angeles, nearly half of the residents are foreign-born. In New York, one-third of the population was born outside the country. With more than one million immigrants from Asia and the Hispanic world entering the U.S. annually, studies are predicting that by the end of the next century, white Americans will be in the minority.

No wonder that with a large and rapidly growing percentage of the population of Asian and Hispanic descent, America is experiencing a sharp increase in marriages of persons of different racial backgrounds. When I was growing up in Massachusetts and Ohio, a "mixed marriage" usually referred to persons of different religious faiths. Mixed-race marriages were rare and frowned upon. When one of my best friends chose to marry a Chinese girl, his father disowned him. But today, there's a rapidly growing acceptance of interracial matrimony. And over the past year, numerous stories concerning "mixed" children have appeared in some of our most widely circulated newspapers and magazines. There's even a magazine–*Interrace*–which features persons of different ethnic backgrounds. Thirty years ago, a Tiger Woods would most likely have considered himself Black--end of story. Today, Tiger points with pride to both his African and Asian ancestors.

Background

I have lived in Hawaii since 1969. I have a daughter, Kimi, who is of Chinese, Swiss, French, English and Welsh descent. My not-always-willing child became the subject of hundreds of my photos. In the years to follow, there was no lack of kids for my camera, as Kim started school, we made friends in a new neighborhood, and my job responsibilities took me around the state.

The idea for *Rainbow Kids* came after discovering *Hawaiian Types* by the renowned photographer, Henry Inn. This 1945 publication presented an assemblage of photos of young Island women with their ethnic backgrounds indicated. The book-jacket noted: "As the reader turns the pages he will be fascinated by the characteristics resulting from the free meeting and mingling of many cultural and racial strains...combining in varying proportions and complexities the blood streams of the five continents and the seven seas." Portions of the book were later published in the national journal, *Colliers*.

In his introduction to this volume, the distinguished sociologist, Andrew Lind, spoke of Hawaii's "most impressive large-scale demonstration of racial democracy at work" and pointed to a "new character, thoroughly Hawaiian and American in spirit" emerging from the mix of many races.

If Lind were to return today, he would not be surprised to learn that Hawaii is leading the way towards a nation of persons, like Tiger Woods, with mixed racial backgrounds. We are accustomed to thinking of American faces as European and Caucasian, but the faces of future generations of Americans are likely to resemble those that will be found in this island state, and within the pages of *Rainbow Kids*.

Rainbow Kids

The 108 "Rainbow Kids" are residents of Hawaii. They live on Oahu, Kauai, Maui, the Big Island and Molokai, and attend both public and private schools. They are most often the children of friends and the classmates of my daughter, and represent the wide variety of ethnic types found in the Islands. They are the sons, daughters and grandchildren of persons of many occupations –

doctors, attorneys, teachers and farmers. It was not necessary to seek models, although some of the Kids have gone on to professional modeling and one (Karen) is presently appearing in national teen magazines.

The photos selected were the best of the 5,000 that I have taken over a 15-year period. In some cases, the Kids have grown into adulthood. One, in fact--Vanessa--has a daughter who is also a Rainbow Kid--Kristoria. Where there is more than one photo of a Kid, the pictures may show him or her at different ages. Some photos show siblings, and the reader may have a good deal of fun trying to guess who they are. Most photos were taken out-of-doors--many at the beach. Children seem to act more naturally outside the house and, after all, this is Hawaii.

I asked the Kids and their parents to list their ethnicities, with the largest percentage first, followed by the second largest, and so forth, and that is how they appear in this book. This was a difficult task for some. One Kid listed her background as "American," having traced her ancestors back to the 18th Century. Many took particular pride in the fact that they were of "Native American" descent (Cherokee, Nipmuc, Algonquin and Ojibwa). One should note that because Kids were not chosen on the basis of their ethnic mix, several groups are under-represented--Samoans, Vietnamese and Thais, for example.

The Kids (with backgrounds noted) represent 34 nations. The most often cited were Chinese (34), followed by English and German (33), Japanese (30), Irish (23), Hawaiian (20), Filipino (17), Scottish (16) and Portuguese (14).

Most of the Kids would refer to themselves by the Hawaiian word *hapa*. *Hapa* is widely used in the Islands to refer to persons of mixed ethnic background. Interestingly, *hapa* is now being used on the Mainland and, perhaps, someday it will be as familiar as *aloha* and *luau*.

Hawaii's Gift

Since the publication of *Hawaiian Types*, America has experienced periods of severe racial strife. As we approach the millennium, we are not witnessing the violent clashes of the 50's and 60's, but occasional incidents remind us that the problem persists.

Are interracial marriages and mixed-race kids the answer? We can not say for sure, but what we do know is this: it is difficult to hate someone of a different ethnicity if that ethnicity is shared by your spouse, your children and your grandchildren!

Perhaps, then, someday Hawaii's greatest attraction will not be its green mountains, lush valleys or sparkling beaches, but its people--and, especially, its *hapa* children. Curt Sanburn, writing in *Honolulu Weekly*, described these children as the Islands' "singular contribution to the evolution of man."

As you get to know the Rainbow Kids through their photographs on the following pages, you may find it difficult to disagree with that statement. They are, I believe, Hawaii's gift to America.

Richard
(6th Grade)

• Swiss
• English
• French
• Welsh

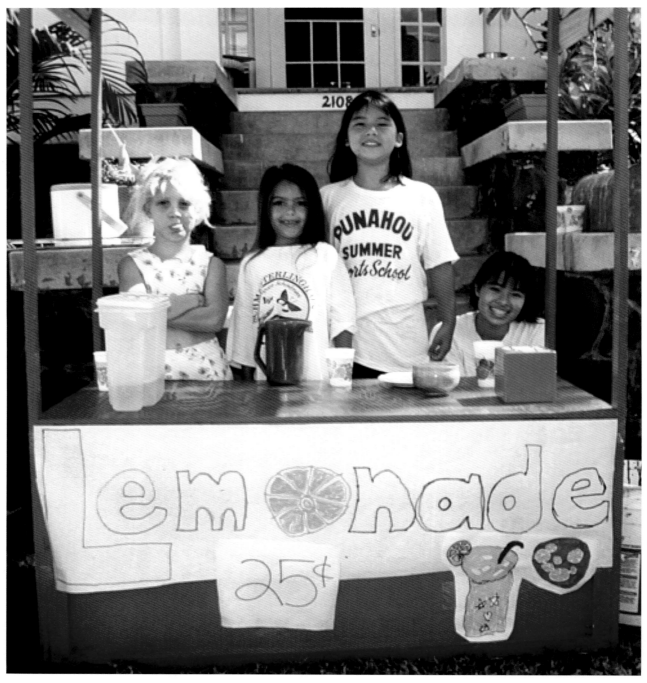

Rebecca, Haley, Leslie and Kimi

Kimo Dan Francisco Chan

Ancestors

Aloha! I'm a rainbow,
A crazy mixed-up kid!
I guess I am the way I am
'Cause what my grandfolks did.

My grandpa on my father's side
Came from southern China.
He married a Hawaiian girl,
With family in Lahaina.

Grandma bore ten children,
Much to my grandpa's joy,
Oriental/Polynesian,
Dad was the youngest boy.

My grandpa on my mother's side
Was born in Baltimore.
When he reached Honolulu,
He opened up a store.

One day a lady wandered in,
With charm and gentle smile.
This lovely Filipina
Would lead Gramps down the aisle.

From this union, there came six:
Tim, Terry, Ted, then Tom,
Tina and Theresa,
And Theresa was my mom.

Me, Jer and Buzzy

I'm a quarter Filipino,
And Caucasian, if you please,
With lots of good Hawaiian blood,
The rest is pure Chinese.

My hair is kinda wavy black,
My eyes are round and blue.
I'm sort of tall for twelve years old,
Girls think I'm cute, it's true!

The local folks are fond of names
That show their ethnic stock.
You choose the one you like the best,
Or use them in a block.

To my friends, I'm known as "Kimo,"
To my Dad, I'm just plain "Dan,"
My Mom likes the name "Francisco,"
And Jer will call me "Chan."

Jeresa is just eight years old,
She has the Chinese looks,
Dark straight hair, and tiny nose
She buries in her books.

Her name is very weird, I know,
But Mom is called "Theresa."
Since Dad is known as "Johnny,"
She ended up "Jeresa"!

Buzzy Sato's my best friend.
We're in the seventh grade.
We like to hang out at the mall,
And surf and rollerblade.

Buzzy's dad is from Japan.
His mom's from Mexico.
Just how they got together,
He doesn't really know.

We wear our caps turned backwards,
With Nike blues and browns,
Baggy shorts and t-shirts--
Jer thinks we look like clowns!

Grinds

You'd love to eat at our house,
Anything you want.
"Adventures in Great Dining"
At our "Chanese" restaurant.

Monday night is Dad's night,
Ono Hawaiian fare,
With pig and poi and laulau,
And lomi salmon there.

Tuesday's Filipino,
And it's Mom's turn to cook.
I love her pork adobo,
But I can't stand balut!

Wednesday night's Jer's favorite,
She thinks this chow is fun,
Sweet and sour spareribs,
With crispy fried wun tun.

Thursday night is my choice,
That's when the family marches
To all-American dining,
Beneath the Golden Arches.

Chicken teriyaki!
We're off to Old Japan,
Saimin and shrimp tempura,
Musubi that's topped with Spam.

We're fond of almost every food,
There's nothing we won't try,
On weekends, it's Korean,
Vietnamese, Laotian, Thai.

I know we're eating far too much
From almost every nation.
Just when I think we'll all explode,
We find a new temptation!

Neighbors

Welcome to our neighborhood,
The folks are all chop sui,
With Kaleikini, Lee, DeLima,
Sapolu, Dill and Lui.

There's Mr. Kaleikini,
Whose name, like mine, is Dan.
You hear him singing day and night,
This one Hawaiian man!

Then there's Jason Scott Lee,
Who "grad" from our high school.
Jer thinks he's really awesome,
I just think he's cool.

Next door's Frank DeLima,
Would you like his autograph?
He's very weird and crazy,
And can really make you laugh.

Jesse Sapolu plays football,
He's big and mean and rough,
But once you get to know him,
You know he's not that tough!

Across the street's an Army man,
Sergeant David Dill.
His roots go back to Africa,
By way of Jacksonville.

Our neighbor, Mrs. Lui,
Uses Feng Shui as a guide.
Her home is pointed to the south,
And painted red inside.

She says that brings good fortune.
I think that may be true,
'Cause she owns a new Mercedes
And a BMW!

New Year's Eve is party time,
When all the neighbors meet,
For shooting firecrackers,
And dancing in the street.

Hawaii
First to cross the ocean,
To these volcanic isles,
Were people from Tahiti,
Who sailed three thousand miles.

It's hard to say when they arrived—
Twelve-hundred years ago?
I asked my history teacher,
Who said she didn't know.

Hawaiians lived here by themselves
'Til seventeen-seventy-eight.
When Captain Cook came cruising in,
And forgot to shut the gate.

Caucasians first, then Chinese,
Cane workers from Japan,
Koreans, Filipinos,
Settled in this land.

Irish, German, Swedish,
Scottish, Portuguese,
Samoan, Puerto Rican,
Thai, Vietnamese.

We're a mix of many cultures,
This is plain to see,
Yet despite our many differences,
We live in harmony.

Yes, everyone is different,
But everyone's the same.
We like to live together,
No matter what our name.

So, when you see a rainbow,
Remember who I am—
A child of Hawaii:
Kimo Dan Francisco Chan!

Back: Makana, Leslie and Jessie. Front: Haley and Alea.

Amy

Japanese • Italian • English • Scottish

Alison

- Slovak
- Hungarian
- Japanese
- Okinawan

17

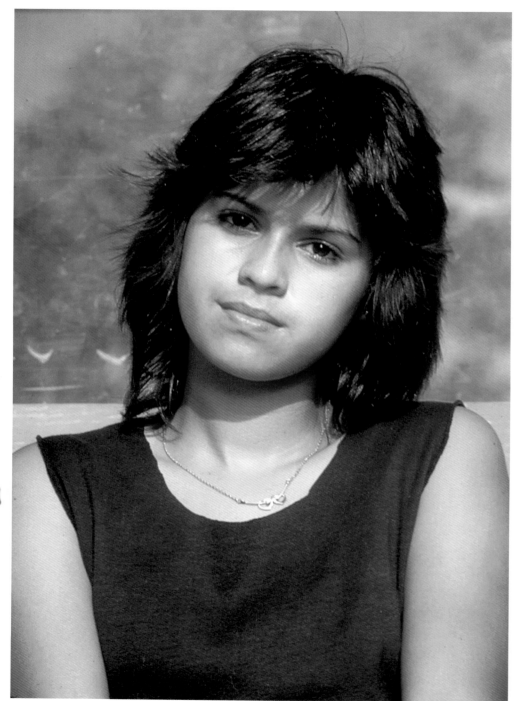

Vanessa

- Japanese
- Portuguese
- Hawaiian
- French
- Irish

Kory and Ryan

Ryan M.

- Japanese
- Chinese
- Filipino

Kimi, Jamie, Jessica and Aileen

Cassandra & Brittany

Korean · English · Hawaiian · German

Joseph W.

- Filipino
- English
- German
- Irish
- Chinese
- Spanish

22

Brittaney

- Hawaiian
- German
- Swedish
- Irish
- Scottish
- Danish

Jaime

Japanese • German

Karen

- Japanese
- English
- Swedish
- German
- Norwegian

Joseph U.

- Japanese
- German
- Swedish
- Irish

Megan

- Japanese
- Swedish
- Italian

Denise

Chinese • Portuguese • Japanese • Cherokee • Korean

Haley

Filipino • English • Chinese • Irish • Spanish

Jasmine K., Christine and Michelle

Nanea

- Irish
- English
- Spanish
- Russian
- Scottish
- Dutch
- Hawaiian
- Cherokee

33

Marie and Kelly

Marie

- Italian
- Portuguese
- English
- French

Jasmine K.

- German
- Italian
- Filipino
- Spanish
- Scottish

35

Ian B.

Korean • English • Chinese • German • Scottish • Swiss

Chloe

Scottish • English • Dutch • German

Cheyne

- Japanese
- German
- Irish
- French

Carolyn

German • Scottish • Irish • Ojibwa • French

Aileen

Japanese • Irish • German • English

Emma

Meghan

Chinese • Jewish

Irish • Japanese • Korean

Kristoria

- Afro-American
- Japanese
- Portuguese
- Hawaiian
- French

Tehani

Hawaiian • Chinese • Irish • Scottish • Filipino • Portuguese

Kevan

Filipino • English

Ryan H.

- Slovak
- Hungarian
- Japanese
- Okinawan

Carissa

- English
- Filipino
- German
- Irish
- Chinese
- Hawaiian

Daughter!

Kimi

- Chinese
- Swiss
- French
- English
- Welsh

47

Kathy

- Japanese
- Okinawan

Jasmine N.

Chinese • Japanese

Christine

- Chinese
- English
- Irish
- Dutch

Kimi and Jasmine N.

Lauren

- Chinese

Miya

- Afro-American
- Japanese
- Cherokee
- French

Maile

- Cook Islands Maori
- English
- Ukrainian
- Mongolian
- Tahitian

52

Kolakiaokalani

- Hawaiian
- Filipino
- Portuguese
- Chinese
- Polish
- German

Kiau

- Irish
- Chinese
- Hawaiian
- Filipino
- Portuguese

Abcde

- Filipino
- Afro-American
- Nipmuc

Allen

- Japanese
- English
- Irish

Lena

- Vietnamese

Janice

- Chinese
- German
- English
- Irish
- Scottish
- French

Chris

- Ukrainian
- Korean
- German

Travis

- Hawaiian
- Chinese
- Irish
- Scottish
- Filipino
- Portuguese

Jaclyn

- Japanese
- Russian
- Okinawan

Trisha & Chelci L.

English • Dutch • Cherokee • German • French

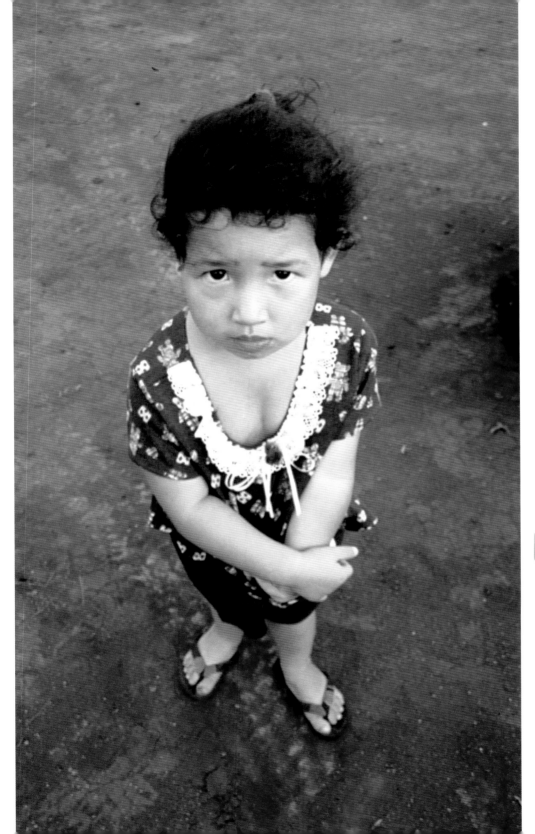

Kamaile

- Hawaiian
- Chinese
- Japanese

Taea

- Japanese
- German
- Irish
- French

Nick

- Chinese
- Danish
- Swedish
- German
- Scottish

Mariah

- Filipino
- English
- German
- Irish
- Chinese
- Spanish

Keoki

- Hawaiian
- Portuguese
- Japanese
- German

Lark

- Hawaiian
- Chinese
- Portuguese
- English
- Scottish

Nanea, Beatrice and Pearl

Matthew

Samoan • French • Algonquin

Kawika

Chinese • Hawaiian • Korean
• Portuguese • English • Spanish

Kiau and Ryan M.

Michael

- Irish
- Italian

Shawna

German • Swedish • Czech

Justin and Abcde

Leslie

Chinese • Okinawan • English • Hawaiian

Ian K.

- Japanese
- Irish

Airika

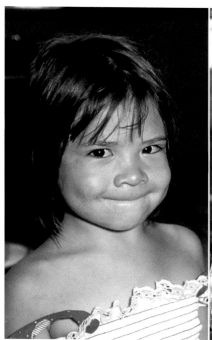

- Scottish
- Pohnpeian
- German
- Japanese
- Filipino

Misha

- Chinese
- English
- German

Sarai

- Hawaiian
- Chinese
- English

Sasha

- Japanese
- Chinese
- Hawaiian
- German

Stephanie

- Polish
- Japanese
- Chinese
- Hawaiian

Mia

- Japanese
- Russian
- English

Kimi, Rebecca, Lindsay, Leslie and Annie

Blair, Rachel and Robyn

Kimi, Blair, Kari and Mariana

(top): Tehani, Travis, Trisha; (middle): Larilyn, Nicholas, Rebecca, Keoni; (bottom): Kiau and Ryan M.

Jordan

- Hawaiian
- Filipino
- Spanish
- Portuguese
- Chinese

Elise

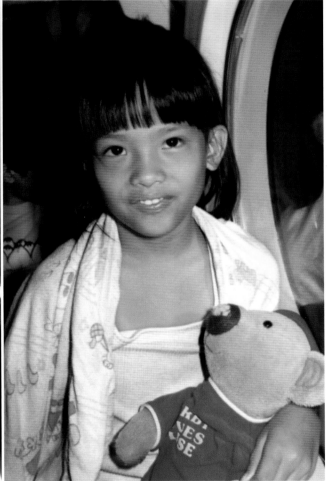

- Filipino
- Chinese

Lindsay

- **English**
- **Scottish**

Mikia

- **Filipino**
- **English**
- **German**
- **Irish**
- **Chinese**
- **Spanish**

Kory

- **Swedish**
- **Filipino**
- **Japanese**
- **Hawaiian**
- **Portuguese**

Leslie and Jodi

Kiyomi and Lauren

Jesse

- Chinese
- Jewish

Jaime, Kristal, Kimi and Emma

Elliott

Chinese • German • English

Alex

Chinese • German • English

Sydney

- Chinese
- German
- English

Tiffany

Japanese • Chinese

Lara

English • German

Carole-Anne

Japanese • Okinawan

Jaclyn

Introduction to Hawaiian Types

by Henry Inn, published by Hastings House in 1945

Andrew W. Lind, Ph.D.
Professor of Sociology
University of Hawaii

Hawaii's color and charm are commonly depicted in the brilliant hues of tropical seas and landscapes. More impressive than the tourist idylls and certainly more fraught with meaning in the long perspective of history is Hawaii's panorama of mingling cultures and of shifting racial types. Thoughtful visitors to the Islands--at least those who have penetrated beyond the banalities of conducted tours and the standardized perfection of beach hotels--have always been fascinated by its colorful mingling of diverse peoples and of contrasted modes of life. Even a century ago, when Honolulu was little more than a small trading center on the long haul of whalers and merchant men across the Pacific, its population was amazingly cosmopolitan and included representatives from over forty scattered regions and nations of the globe. Within the present century, social scientists have come to regard Hawaii as one of the foremost observatories of the world in which to investigate what actually happens when sharply contrasted cultures and races meet. Some observers claim to have found in Hawaii's careless disregard for color lines one of the most eloquent and convincing answers to the racial bigotry and exclusiveness which threatens to become the world's worst headache in our generation. Certain it is that Hawaii of 1944 offers America's most impressive large scale demonstration of racial democracy at work.

To capture in permanent and visible form something of the human charm derived from the free meeting and mingling of many cultural and racial strains in Hawaii was a prime objective of this book. All of the more usual "pure" ethnic stocks which an expanding commercial and plantation economy has brought together in these islands--Chinese, Japanese, Korean, Filipino and Caucasian--are pleasingly represented; but even more impressive is the remarkable array of hybrid types, combining in varying proportions and complexities the blood streams of the five continents and seven seas. The one unifying racial strain in most of the hybrid types, as it is also of the group which is destined to become Hawaii's largest in the not distant future, is, appropriately, Polynesian.

This is, however, no ordinary collection of anthropological types. No effort, in fact, was made to secure a statistical sampling of physical types, nor to guarantee a completely accurate reporting of the ancestries in some of the racial hybrids. The people of mixed ancestry in Hawaii, like elsewhere in the world, sometimes forgot minor racial antecedents which do not enjoy the highest prestige in the community. The author, with the artist's subtle sense for what is expressive of the kaleidoscopic life of the Islands and with the studied skill of a seasoned professional, has performed a service of which the scientist and his calipers and slide rules, may well be envious.

The kamaaina (old timer) resident of Hawaii will readily recognize the common racial masks which appear on the faces of the "pure bloods" and of a few of the mixed bloods typified in the collection--masks difficult to describe in the language of the layman, but adequately revealed by the camera in the configurations of head form and facial casts. But even the oldest kamaaina and the most experienced student of physical anthropology will be baffled by the question as to the precise racial ancestry of not only most of the types represented in this collection, but also of an increasing proportion of Hawaii's entire population.

The reason for this confusion is partly, of course, the growing tendency for marriages to occur across racial lines in Hawaii and for the resulting offspring to share the biological heritage of two or more racial groups. Nearly one quarter of all children born within recent years in the Islands are of mixed racial ancestry. But another reason, clearly evident in the photographs themselves, is the growing congruity in appearance between peoples of different racial extractions who are subjected to the unifying influences of Island life.

It is as though the racial and ancestral masks were becoming slowly transparent and a new character, thoroughly Hawaiian and American in spirit, were forcing itself through to dominant expression. Nor is it merely the superficial transforma-

tion of a Hollywood coiffure or a Hawaiian aloha shirt. Facial muscles have become more relaxed and an expressiveness of countenance, born of long experience in Hawaii's free and democratic atmosphere, has supplanted the inflexible facial cast of the Oriental and European immigrant pioneers. The faces in this book, whatever else they may be because of the varied racial uniforms, are also typically American. With an accuracy of its own, the camera has helped to document the fact that by various routes the many and varied races of the world are becoming in Hawaii "one people."

Kimi

Rainbow Kids' Quiz

1. *Two sisters and a brother. Can you name them?*
2. *Which Kid is the mother of Kristoria?*
3. *If you don't watch out, this Kid might squirt you!*
4. *Name the Kids who are eating a coconut.*
5. *In the bottom photo on page 79, two of the girls are sisters. Which ones?*
6. *This Kid has ancestors who came from Poland and China.*
7. *Which Kid is Emma's brother?*
8. *Can you name the live animals the Kids are holding?*
9. *These Kids are part Cherokee.*
10. *There are two sets of identical twins. Name them.*
11. *This Kid is definitely a football fan.*
12. *This Kid is part Algonquin.*
13. *On page 60, which Kid (on the rope) is looking directly at the camera?*
14. *Who is Sevi's sister?*
15. *He's Tehani's brother.*
16. *Which Kid is Alison's brother?*
17. *Which Kid has a parent who came from Micronesia?*
18. *Two brothers and a sister. Name them.*
19. *Which Kids are wearing candy leis?*
20. *Can you name all of the sisters?*

Kids' Quiz Answers

1. *Mariah, Mikia and Joseph*
2. *Vanessa (photo taken when she was 15)*
3. *Lindsay*
4. *Haley and Rebecca*
5. *Rachel and Robyn*
6. *Stephanie*
7. *Jesse*
8. *Rabbit, dog, hamster, cat and mouse*
9. *Nanea, Denise, Miya, Trisha and Chelci L.*
10. *Trisha and Chelci L., Cassandra and Brittany*
11. *Aileen*
12. *Matthew*
13. *Sasha*
14. *Najeda*
15. *Travis*
16. *Ryan H.*
17. *Airika*
18. *Elliott, Alex and Sydney*
19. *Ian K. and Tiffany*
20. *Cassandra and Brittany; Christine and Michelle; Larilyn and Trisha; Trisha and Chelci L.; Mariah and Mikia; Nanea, Beatrice and Pearl; Rachel and Robyn*

Rainbow Kids
Index

Kid/page number of photo or photos

Abcde 55, 73
Aileen 20, 40
Airika....................................77
Alea.....................................15
Alexander..............................86
Alison 17
Allen 55
Alvaro 4, 39
Amy 4, 16
Andrew....................................4
Annie....................................79
Beatrice 63
Blair 79, 80
Brian 37, 67
Brittaney 23
Brittany 21
Carissa.................................46
Carole-Anne 89
Carolyn 40
Cassandra 21
Chelci 58
Cheyne 26, 37, 39, 67
Chloe....................................38
Christine 32, 50
Chris.....................................57
Denise.............2, 4, 28, 29
Elise 81
Elliott....................................86
Emma 5, 41, 85
Haley.....cover, 12, 15, 30, 31, 67
Ian B. 36
Ian K. 76
Jaclyn 57, 90
Jaime.................4, 5, 24, 85
Jamie 20
Janice....................................56

Jasmine K. 32, 35
Jasmine N.........................49, 51
Jennifer.................................26
Jesse 84
Jessie 15
Jessica 20
Jodi 83
Jordan 81
Joseph U. 27
Joseph W. 22
Justin 73
Kamaile 59
Karen 25
Kari.......................................80
Kathy 48
Kawika 64
Kelly.....................................34
Keoki 62
Keoni 80
Kevan 45
Kiau.........back cover, 54, 65, 80
Kimi 4, 5, 12, 20, 27,
            47, 51, 79, 80, 85, 92
Kiyomi...................................83
Kolakiaokalani 53
Kory 4, 19, 82
Kristal 85
Kristoria .....back cover, 5, 42, 43
Lara 88
Larilyn 80
Lark 62
Lauren 52, 83
Lena 55
Leslie ....back cover, 8, 12,
            15, 74, 75, 79, 83
Lindsay 61, 79, 82
Maile 52

Makana 15
Mariah...................................62
Mariana..................................80
Marie 34
Matthew.................................64
Megan 27
Meghan 27, 41, 61
Mia 78
Michael 66
Michelle 32
Mikia.....................................82
Misha 77
Miya 52
Najeda 70, 71
Nanea 33, 63
Nicholas 80
Nick 60
Pearl 63
Rachel 79
Rebecca A. 80
Rebecca R. 12, 67, 68, 69, 79
Robyn 79
Ryan H. 46
Ryan M..............4, 19, 65, 80
Sarai 77
Sasha.................27, 60, 78
Sevi 70
Shawna 72
Stephanie.........................61, 78
Sydney 87
Taea......................................60
Tehani 44, 80
Tiffany 88
Travis 57, 80
Trisha A. 80
Trisha L. 58
Vanessa.................................18

About the poet/photographer

C. Richard Fassler, who speaks six languages fluently, has experienced a variety of cultures around the world. After graduation from Kenyon College in Ohio in 1963, he lived in France, Germany, Thailand (Peace Corps) and Indonesia before returning to the U.S. to take an M.A. degree in International Education from Columbia University. Following graduation, he taught in American Samoa and the Philippines.

Mr. Fassler has been a resident of Hawaii for the past 26 years, during which time he has been an employee of the Aquaculture Development Program of the State Department of Land & Natural Resources, and more recently, the Department of Business, Economic Development & Tourism, and a part-time organic arugula farmer.

As a writer, Mr. Fassler has authored and edited over 70 publications in the field of aquaculture. He is considered a world-expert in the cultivation of pearls. Hawaii residents are familiar with his frequent contributions to Letters to the Editor of *The Honolulu Advertiser* and the *Honolulu Star-Bulletin*. In the "Viewpoint" and "Commentary" sections of both newspapers, he has discussed subjects ranging from pearl farming and crime prevention to the restoration of the monarchy. In 1997, he was the recipient of a Golden Letter Award from the *Honolulu Star-Bulletin*.

As a photographer, Mr. Fassler's greatest interest has been in photographing children. His photographs have been published in aquaculture trade publications, *Midweek Magazine*, and *The Toledo Blade*.

As a poet, Mr. Fassler has published 10 humorous poems in *The Honolulu Advertiser*, the *Honolulu Star-Bulletin* and *Midweek Magazine*.

Mr. Fassler resides in Manoa Valley and serves as a member of the Manoa Neighborhood Board.